YOUR MONEY YOUR FUTURE

A STUDENT'S GUIDE TO FINANCIAL SUCCESS

By

Nick Imoru

Achievers Publishing
Calgary, Canada

YOUR MONEY, YOUR FUTURE: A STUDENT'S GUIDE TO FINANCIAL SUCCESS

ISBN: 978-1-989291-13-9

Published in Canada, by
Achievers Publishing

Canadian Cataloguing in Publication (CIP)
A Record of this Publication is available from the Library and Archives Canada (LAC).

For further information or permission, address:
Achievers Publishing
Calgary, Canada
E-mail: info@achieverspublishing.com
www.achieverspublishing.com

Printed in Canada for Achievers Publishing

YOUR MONEY YOUR FUTURE

A STUDENT'S GUIDE TO FINANCIAL SUCCESS

Dedication

This book is dedicated to all the students I have had the privilege to mentor and teach at **Achievers Institute.**

Your curiosity, resilience, and drive for excellence have been a source of inspiration. It has been an honor to guide you on your journey toward academic success and personal growth.

May this book serve as a tool to empower you to take control of your finances, secure your future, and achieve your dreams. Remember, your potential is limitless—keep striving, keep learning, and keep achieving!

Table of Contents

Contents

INTRODUCTION: WHY FINANCIAL LITERACY MATTERS

Understanding the Importance of Managing Money Early

Financial literacy is the foundation of a successful and independent life. From a young age, the decisions you make about your money can shape your future. Learning how to manage money effectively helps you avoid common financial pitfalls such as debt, poor credit scores, or even living paycheck to paycheck.

By understanding how money works and taking control of your finances early on, you set yourself up for success, whether it's saving for a major purchase like a new laptop, college tuition, or even your first car. The sooner you start, the more confident you'll feel about managing your money as you grow older.

Imagine building a strong foundation for your financial future by taking small but important steps now. With the right financial habits, you'll be prepared to handle the twists and turns life throws your way. You'll make smarter decisions about where your money goes and be in control of your financial destiny. Managing your money early empowers you to plan for both the present and future.

Setting Financial Goals

One of the most powerful ways to manage your money is by setting clear financial goals. These goals give you a sense of purpose, direction, and motivation. There are two main types of financial goals: short-term and long-term.

Short-Term Goals are objectives you aim to achieve in the near future. This might include saving up for a new pair of shoes, a video game, or attending a concert. These are things that can typically be achieved within a few weeks or months. Short-term goals help you practice discipline and budgeting on a smaller scale, which prepares you for larger financial milestones down the road.

Long-Term Goals require a more extended period to achieve and usually involve bigger financial commitments. Examples include saving for college, buying a car, or even starting a business. These goals take several years and require more consistent saving and financial planning. By breaking down your long-term goals into smaller, achievable steps, you'll have a roadmap to get you to where you want to be financially.

Setting both short-term and long-term goals keep you motivated and on track. Your short-term achievements provide quick wins and confidence boosts, while your long-term goals give you something to work toward, knowing that the rewards are worth the wait.

Overview of Key Financial Skills

Mastering financial literacy means developing a set of key skills that will serve you for life. Each of these skills builds on the others, creating a full picture of what it means to manage your money well.

1. **Earning:** The journey starts with learning how to earn money. Whether through part-time jobs,

entrepreneurial ventures, or eventually through your career, understanding how to make money is the first step. It's not just about working hard, but also about using your talents, skills, and interests to create income. Earning gives you the resources you need to begin building your financial future.

2. **Saving:** Once you've earned money, the next crucial step is saving it. Saving ensures that you have funds available for emergencies, future goals, and bigger purchases. It's about discipline—setting aside a portion of what you earn for future needs rather than spending it all immediately. The power of saving lies in the fact that small, consistent contributions over time can lead to significant financial growth, especially when you take advantage of interest.

3. **Budgeting:** Creating a budget is like making a plan for your money. It helps you manage where your money goes by balancing your income and expenses. With a budget, you can make sure you're covering your needs (like food, transportation, or school supplies) while still

leaving room for your wants (like entertainment or saving for new gadgets). A budget helps prevent overspending and ensures you're on track to meet your financial goals.

4. **Spending:** Learning how to spend wisely is an essential skill. Everyone spends money, but making smart spending choices can help you stretch your budget further. This means making informed decisions about whether to buy something, comparison shopping, and knowing when it's better to save money rather than spend it on unnecessary things.

5. **Borrowing:** In life, there may be times when you will need to borrow money to achieve a goal, whether it's going to college, buying a car, or investing in something important. Borrowing responsibly means understanding loans, interest rates, and how to repay what you owe without damaging your financial future. Having a good understanding of how to manage debt ensures that borrowing works for you, not against you.

6. **Protecting:** Keeping your money safe is just as important as earning it. Whether it's protecting your money from theft, online fraud, or making sure you don't lose important financial documents, being financially responsible means taking steps to safeguard your assets. This also includes keeping personal information private and making sure you have access to your money when you need it.

7. **Giving:** Financial success isn't just about personal gain. Giving is an essential part of the financial picture. Whether it's donating money to a cause you care about, helping others in need, or supporting community initiatives, giving helps make the world a better place. Including giving in your financial plan allows you to make a positive impact on society, and it can be a rewarding part of your financial journey.

In this guide, you'll learn how to master each of these skills so that you can build a bright financial future. With time and practice, managing money will become second nature, and you'll have the knowledge and confidence to make smart financial choices that serve you well for years to come.

CHAPTER 1: LEARNING TO EARN

Recognizing and Developing Your Skills for Future Success

Everyone has unique skills and talents that, when developed and applied, can lead to financial success. Learning to earn money starts with understanding your strengths and interests. Some people are naturally good at solving problems, others excel in creative arts, while some are great with numbers or communication. Recognizing what you're good at and how you can turn that into a source of income is the first step toward building a financially independent future.

Take a moment to reflect on your skills and passions. What are you naturally good at? Do you enjoy helping people? Are you passionate about technology? Maybe you have a talent for making art or a gift for working with animals. By identifying these strengths, you can start to think about ways to turn them into opportunities to earn money. The key is to find something that not only earns you money but also motivates and excites you.

Developing your skills requires time, practice, and sometimes formal education. If you are passionate about something, it's important to invest time in improving those abilities. The more you refine your talents, the more valuable you become in the job market or as an entrepreneur. Whether it's learning a new language, mastering a musical instrument, or developing computer skills, the effort you put into enhancing your talents will pay off in the long run.

Identifying Potential Part-Time Jobs or Entrepreneurial Ventures

As a student, there are many opportunities you have to start earning money, even before you finish school. Part-time jobs and entrepreneurial ventures are great ways to gain financial independence while also gaining valuable work experience.

Part-Time Jobs can be a flexible way to start earning money. Common options for students include working in retail, at restaurants, babysitting, tutoring, or even freelancing in areas like graphic design or writing. These jobs provide a steady income and help you develop important skills such as time management, communication, and customer service. A part-time job can also help you get a sense of what kind of work environment you enjoy, which will be helpful as you think about your future career.

On the other hand, **Entrepreneurship** offers a chance to create something of your own and potentially earn even more money. If you have a specific talent, hobby, or passion, you might consider turning it into a business. For example, if you love baking, you could start a small business selling homemade treats to friends, family, or neighbors. If you are skilled in a particular subject, you might offer tutoring services to other students. Entrepreneurship allows you to set your own hours, be your own boss, and develop a deeper understanding of how businesses work. Many successful entrepreneurs started small, so don't be afraid to take that first step.

Some questions to help you brainstorm:

- What part-time jobs are available in your area that align with your skills?
- What business could you start with little capital and your current abilities?
- How can you turn your hobbies into a source of income?

Importance of Education and Skill-Building for Career Advancement

In today's world, education and skill development are key to unlocking higher-paying opportunities. While you can start earning money early with part-time jobs or small businesses, continuing your education and acquiring new skills will help you advance in your career and increase your earning potential over time.

Formal education, such as completing high school and pursuing higher education (college, trade school, or professional certifications), opens doors to more specialized and higher-paying careers. For example, careers in fields like medicine, engineering, law, or technology often require years of education and training, but they also come with high earning potential. Even if you don't pursue a traditional college path, there are many ways to acquire valuable skills through trade schools, online courses, or apprenticeships.

Aside from formal education, **skill-building** is crucial for career advancement. The world is constantly changing, especially with new technologies emerging every day. Keeping your skills up to date, whether through coding, marketing, writing, or public speaking, is an investment in your future. Employers look for people who are adaptable, willing to learn, and capable of solving new problems. By continually improving yourself, you make sure that you stay competitive in the job market and can take advantage of new opportunities.

Remember, the more you know and the more skills you have, the more valuable you become to potential employers or customers. Education and skill-building are investments in yourself that pay dividends over the course of your lifetime.

Exploring Career Paths and Their Earning Potential

There are countless career paths you can take, each with different earning potentials and growth opportunities. While it's important to choose a career that aligns with your interests and skills, it's also essential to consider the financial side of things. Some careers offer higher salaries but may require more years of education or training, while others may have lower starting salaries but allow for quicker entry into the workforce.

Here are a few factors to consider when exploring career paths:

- **Earning Potential:** Some careers, such as those in STEM (Science, Technology, Engineering, and Math) fields, healthcare, or business, tend to offer higher salaries. On the other hand, careers in the arts, education, or nonprofit work may start with lower salaries but offer other forms of rewards, such as job satisfaction or opportunities for creative expression.

- **Job Demand:** Careers in growing industries, like technology or renewable energy, are more likely to offer job security and opportunities for advancement. Researching which careers that are in high demand can help you make informed decisions about your future.

- **Work-Life Balance:** It's also important to think about what kind of lifestyle you want. Some careers may offer high pay but require long hours or frequent travels, while others may offer more flexibility but with a lower salary.

Take the time to research different career paths, including what kind of education or training is required, what the job involves on a daily basis, and what the average salary is. This will help you make informed decisions about your future and give you a clear idea of what you want to achieve.

You don't have to decide on a career right away, but it's good to start thinking about it early. Explore different options by talking to professionals, participating in internships, or taking classes in areas that interest you. The more you explore, the better prepared you'll be to make decisions about your career and earning potential.

By recognizing your talents, exploring job options, and investing in your education and skill development, you'll be well on your way to earning your own money and building a strong financial future.

CHAPTER 2: SAVING FOR A SECURE FUTURE

Understanding the Habit of "Paying Yourself First"

The concept of "paying yourself first" is one of the most important habits you can develop when it comes to managing your money. It simply means that before you spend your money on anything else, you set aside a portion of your earnings for savings. This habit ensures that saving becomes a priority, not an afterthought.

Why is this important? Most people make the mistake of spending first and saving whatever is left over—if anything at all. By making saving the first thing you do when you get paid, you ensure that you're building a financial cushion for the future, even if it's just a small amount at a time.

Think of "paying yourself first" as a way to protect your future self. Whether you're saving for a rainy day, a new gadget, or a bigger goal like college tuition, setting aside money consistently will help you reach those goals faster. Plus, the earlier you start, the more your savings can grow, especially with the help of compound interest (more on that later).

To make this habit easy, consider automating your savings. You can set up automatic transfers from your checking account to your savings account so that every time you get paid, a portion of your income goes directly into savings without you even having to think about it. The key is to make saving a regular, non-negotiable part of your financial routine.

Differentiating Between Savings Goals

Not all savings goals are the same. Some goals can be achieved in a few weeks, while others might take years of consistent saving. Understanding the difference between short-term, medium-term, and long-term savings goals will help you create a plan that works for you and keeps you motivated to stick with it.

- **Short-Term Goals** are things you want to achieve within a few weeks or months. These could include saving for a concert ticket, a new book, or even a small trip with friends. Short-term goals are usually smaller in scale, but they're important because they keep you focused and help you practice saving regularly. These goals give you a quick sense of accomplishment, which can motivate you to save for bigger things.

- **Medium-Term Goals** are typically set for anywhere between a few months to a year. Examples of medium-term goals might include saving for a new laptop, holiday spending money, or an upgraded smartphone. These goals require a bit more patience and planning but are achievable within a reasonable time frame.

- **Long-Term Goals** are the biggest goals and often take several years to achieve. These might include saving for college, buying a car, or even starting a small business. Long-term goals require more commitment, but the rewards are greater. To reach these goals, you'll need to break them down into smaller, manageable steps and stay consistent with your saving habits.

By identifying what you're saving for and categorizing those goals into short-term, medium-term, and long-term, you can prioritize where your money should go and how long it will take to reach each milestone. For example, you may decide to save 20% of your earnings for a short-term goal, 30% for a medium-term goal, and 50% for a long-term goal. This way, you can work toward multiple objectives at the same time without neglecting any of them.

Compound Interest: How Your Money Grows Over Time

One of the most powerful tools at your disposal when it comes to saving money is compound interest. Compound interest means that you not only earn interest on the money you save but also on the interest that your savings generate. Over time, this creates a snowball effect, where your savings grow faster and faster.

Let's break it down. Suppose you put $100 into a savings account that earns 1% interest per year. After one year, you would have $101—your original $100 plus $1 in interest. In the second year, you would earn 1% interest not only on your original $100 but also on the $1 of interest from the first year, giving you $102.01. As the years go by, the interest you earn compounds, meaning you earn interest on both your initial savings and the interest it has already earned.

The earlier you start saving, the more time compound interest has to work its magic. Even if you're only able to save small amounts at first, over time, those small amounts can grow into significant sums, thanks to compound interest. The longer you leave your money in a savings account, the more it will grow.

Example: If you save $50 per month in an account that earns 1% interest compounded monthly, here's what your savings might look like after three years:

- After Year 1: $603.26

- After Year 2: $1,212.58

- After Year 3: $1,828.02

While the interest rate in this example is low, many savings and investment accounts offer higher interest rates, especially over the long term. The key takeaway is that compound interest rewards consistency and patience. The more you save and the longer you let your money sit in your account, the more you'll earn without any extra effort on your part.

Practical Tips for Building a Savings Plan Early On

Saving doesn't have to be complicated. With a few practical steps, you can create a savings plan that works for you and helps you reach your financial goals. Here are some tips to help you get started:

1. **Set Clear Goals**

   The first step to building a savings plan is knowing what you're saving for. Write down your short-term, medium-term, and long-term goals and decide how much money you'll need for each one. Having clear goals will keep you motivated and focused.

2. **Create a Budget**

A budget helps you see where your money is going and ensures that you have enough left over to save. Track your income and expenses, and then decide how much of your earnings you can set aside for savings each month. Try to prioritize saving at least 10-20% of your income.

3. **Start Small, Be Consistent**

Even if you can't save a lot right away, it's important to start with whatever you can and make it a habit. If you save $5 a week, that's $260 by the end of the year. The key is to be consistent—over time, small amounts will add up.

4. **Automate Your Savings**

One of the easiest ways to ensure that you save regularly is by setting up automatic transfers to your savings account. This way, a portion of your income goes directly into savings without you having to think about it. Automating your savings makes it easier to stay disciplined and reach your goals.

5. **Separate Your Savings**

To avoid the temptation of spending your savings, keep your savings account separate from your checking account. This helps prevent accidental spending and ensures that your savings are there when you need them.

6. **Review and Adjust**

Regularly review your savings plan to see how you're progressing. If you receive a raise, allowance increase, or other forms of income, consider increasing the amount you save. Similarly, if your expenses change, adjust your savings contributions accordingly.

Building a solid saving habit is one of the best ways to secure your financial future. By paying yourself first, setting clear goals, and understanding the power of compound interest, you can ensure that your money is working for you over time. The earlier you start, the more you'll benefit, so take charge of your savings plan today.

CHAPTER 3: BUILDING A BUDGET

Defining a Budget and Understanding Needs vs. Wants

At the heart of smart money management is the ability to budget. A budget is a plan that helps you manage your income, track your expenses, and ensure that you're putting your money toward your financial goals. In simple terms, a budget tells you where your money is going and helps you make sure it's being spent wisely.

But before you can create an effective budget, it's important to understand the difference between needs and wants. This is key to making informed decisions about where to allocate your money.

- **Needs** are the essentials you can't live without. These include things like food, shelter, transportation, school supplies, and clothing. Needs are non-negotiable expenses that you must cover to ensure your well-being and day-to-day functioning.

- **Wants**, on the other hand, are things you would like to have but can live without. These include things like eating out at restaurants, going to the movies, buying new gadgets, or getting the latest fashion trends. While these items may bring happiness, they are not essential for survival, and they should be prioritized only after your needs are met.

A successful budget ensures that your needs are taken care of first. Then, if there is money left over, you can decide how to allocate it to your wants or toward your savings goals. Striking a balance between needs and wants is the cornerstone of smart financial decision-making.

Creating a Personalized Budget to Track Income and Expenses

Creating your own budget is the next step in taking control of your finances. A personalized budget gives you a clear picture of how much money you have coming in, how much is going out, and where you can make adjustments. Here's a simple guide to help you create your own budget:

1. **Calculate Your Income**

   Start by listing all sources of income. This might include:

   - Allowance from your parents

   - Money from part-time jobs or side gigs

   - Gifts, scholarships, or any other income

   Total up all your sources of income for the month. This gives you a starting point for your budget.

2. **List Your Expenses**

   Next, track all your expenses. This includes both fixed expenses (those that stay the same each month) and variable expenses (those that change from month to month). Examples include:

- **Fixed expenses:** Rent, subscriptions, transportation, savings

- **Variable expenses:** Groceries, entertainment, dining out, personal spending

Categorize each expense as a **need** or a **want** to help you understand where your money is going.

3. **Compare Income and Expenses**

Subtract your total expenses from your total income. If you have money left over, you're in good shape! This extra money can be allocated toward savings or spent on your wants. If your expenses are greater than your income, you'll need to find ways to reduce your spending.

4. **Make Adjustments**

Based on the comparison of your income and expenses, decide where you can cut back. Are there unnecessary expenses that you can reduce or eliminate? Are there areas where you can save more? Adjust your spending so that your budget aligns with your goals.

5. **Set Your Goals**

   Once your basic needs are covered, prioritize your goals. Decide how much money you want to allocate toward short-term, medium-term, and long-term goals. This helps keep you motivated and ensures that you're making progress toward your financial dreams.

Your budget should be flexible and adaptable. Life changes, and so will your income and expenses. Review your budget regularly and make adjustments as needed to stay on track.

Adjusting Your Spending Habits to Meet Saving Goals

To achieve your financial goals, you'll need to make conscious decisions about how you spend your money. Adjusting your spending habits may seem challenging at first, but it's a crucial step in meeting your saving goals.

Here are some strategies to help you adjust your spending habits:

1. **Prioritize Needs Over Wants**

   Before making any purchase, ask yourself: Is this a need or a want? By focusing on your needs first, you'll ensure that your essential expenses are covered before spending money on things you can live without. This discipline will free up more money for savings and long-term goals.

2. **Cut Back on Small, Unnecessary Expenses**

   Small expenses, like buying coffee every day or spending money on snacks, can add up over time. Identify areas where you're spending unnecessarily and look for ways to cut back. For example, making coffee at home or packing a lunch can save you hundreds of dollars over the course of a year.

3. **Use Cash Instead of Credit**

When you use cash, you're more aware of how much you're spending, and it's easier to stick to your budget. Credit cards, on the other hand, can make it easy to overspend. If possible, pay with cash or with a debit card so that you only spend what you have.

4. **Create a "Fun Money" Fund**

It's important to enjoy your money too! Allocate a small portion of your income toward fun activities or treats for yourself but set a limit. Having a designated amount for fun spending helps you stay within your budget while still enjoying life.

5. **Track Your Progress**

Regularly review your budget and savings plan to track your progress. Celebrate small wins along the way, whether it's saving for a concert ticket or reaching a milestone in your college fund. Tracking your progress will keep you motivated and help you stay committed to your financial goals.

By making small adjustments to your spending habits, you'll free up more money for savings without feeling like you're depriving yourself.

Case Studies of Budget Plans

Let's take a look at some real-life examples of budget plans for different financial goals.

Short-Term Budget Plan:

Goal: Save $100 for a new book within one month.

Income: $50 per week from a part-time job = $200 per month

Budget Breakdown:

- Fixed expenses (transportation, school supplies): $50

- Variable expenses (lunches, entertainment): $100

- Savings for book: $50

In this case, you can comfortably cover your fixed and variable expenses and set aside $50 for your short-term goal, reaching your $100 savings goal in two months.

Medium-Term Budget Plan:

Goal: Save $600 for a new laptop in six months.

Income: $75 per week from tutoring = $300 per month

Budget Breakdown:

- Fixed expenses (phone bill, transportation): $100
- Variable expenses (personal spending, entertainment): $100
- Savings for laptop: $100

With a consistent savings plan, you can save $100 per month and reach your goal of $600 in six months without sacrificing your essential expenses.

Long-Term Budget Plan:

Goal: Save $3,000 for college tuition in two years.

Income: $150 per week from a part-time job = $600 per month

Budget Breakdown:

- Fixed expenses (rent, utilities, transportation): $300

- Variable expenses (entertainment, personal spending): $150

- Savings for college: $150

By consistently saving $150 per month, you'll accumulate $3,600 in two years—enough to cover your long-term goal of $3,000 for college tuition, with some extra for unexpected expenses.

Creating a budget isn't just about controlling your money—it's about giving yourself the freedom to reach your goals. Whether you're saving for something small like a new gadget or planning for bigger expenses like college, a well-structured budget helps you stay on track and feel confident about your financial future.

CHAPTER 4: SMART SPENDING

How to Make Wise Purchasing Decisions Through Comparison Shopping

Spending wisely is a skill that can save you a significant amount of money over time. One of the best ways to ensure that you're getting the most value for your money is through **comparison shopping**. This involves researching and comparing different options before making a purchase to find the best deal available.

Comparison shopping helps you make informed decisions by:

- **Evaluating Prices:** Different stores or online retailers often sell the same product at varying prices. Before buying, check multiple sources to see where you can get the best price. It's easy to assume that the first price you see is the best, but a little research can sometimes save you a significant amount of money.

- **Checking Quality:** It's not just about the price—quality matters too. You may find two similar items at different prices, but the cheaper one may not last as long. When comparing products, consider factors like durability, warranties, and user reviews. Sometimes, spending a little more upfront can save you money in the long run if the product lasts longer.

- **Looking for Deals and Discounts:** Before making a purchase, check for any available coupons, promotions, or discounts. Many stores offer seasonal sales, student discounts, or membership perks that can lower the price. Additionally, some online retailers offer price-matching policies, so if you find a better deal elsewhere, they might match that price.

- For example, if you're buying a new pair of shoes, rather than purchasing the first pair you see, compare different brands, check multiple stores, and read reviews to make sure you're getting the best deal for your budget. Comparison shopping takes a little extra time but can save you a lot of money in the long run.

Understanding the Difference Between Brand Names and Generic Products

When you're shopping, you'll often encounter two main categories of products: **brand-name** products and **generic** (or store-brand) products. While brand-name items are often more well-known and heavily advertised, generic products are typically much cheaper. But is the higher price of brand-name products always worth it?

- **Brand-Name Products:** These are products made by companies that are often household names. They typically come with recognizable logos and packaging. Brand-name products are sometimes associated with higher quality, but this is not always the case. In many situations, you're paying more for the name, advertising, and packaging rather than the actual quality of the product.

- **Generic Products:** These are usually the store's own brand or a less well-known alternative. Generic products often have similar ingredients or materials as their brand-name counterparts but are sold at a lower price because they aren't as heavily advertised. For example, generic cereals, medicines, and cleaning products can be just as effective as their brand-name versions but cost significantly less.

It's important to recognize that while brand-name products might be better in some cases, they aren't always necessary. Many generic products meet the same standards of quality, and you can save a lot of money by opting for them. As a smart shopper, knowing when to choose a brand name versus a generic option is key to keeping more money in your pocket.

Tip: When in doubt, check the labels. If the ingredients or specifications are the same, there's often no reason to pay extra for the brand-name version.

Prioritizing Essential Spending and Avoiding Impulse Buys

Impulse buying—making unplanned, spur-of-the-moment purchases—is one of the easiest ways to derail your budget. We've all been there: you're at the store to pick up one item, but then you spot something you didn't plan to buy, and before you know it, it's in your cart. While an occasional treat is okay, making a habit of impulse buying can quickly eat into your savings.

Here's how to avoid impulse buys and focus on **prioritizing essential spending**:

1. **Make a List and Stick to It**

   One of the simplest ways to prevent impulse purchases is to go shopping with a list. Write down the items you need to buy, whether it's groceries, school supplies, or clothes. When you're in the store, stick to that list and avoid wandering into aisles you don't need to be in. If something catches your eye that's not on the list, pause and ask yourself if it's truly necessary.

2. **Delay the Purchase**

If you're tempted by an impulse buy, give yourself a 24-hour waiting period. This gives you time to think about whether you really need the item or if it was just an emotional decision in the moment. Often, you'll find that after some time has passed, the urge to buy the item fades, and you realize you didn't need it after all.

3. **Differentiate Between Needs and Wants**

When you're about to make a purchase, take a moment to categorize the item as a need or a want. Essential spending should always take priority. Needs include things like food, school supplies, and transportation, while wants are non-essential items like the latest gadget, fashionable clothes, or a spontaneous outing with friends. By consciously prioritizing your needs, you'll have more money left over for savings and long-term goals.

4. **Set a Budget for Fun Spending**

It's important to enjoy your money too, so give yourself a small budget for non-essential or "fun" spending each month. This way, you can treat yourself to things you want, like going to the movies or buying a new game, without feeling guilty. The key is to set a limit and not exceed it. Once that portion of your budget is used up, resist the urge to spend more.

By making mindful spending decisions and avoiding impulse purchases, you'll have more control over your money and be able to focus on meeting your financial goals.

How Spending Decisions Impact Long-Term Savings

Every spending decision you make today has an impact on your financial future. It's easy to think that small purchases here and there don't make a big difference, but over time, those small expenses add up and can affect your ability to save for larger goals.

For example, imagine you spend $10 a week on snacks or small impulse purchases. That might not seem like much at the time, but over a month, that adds up to $40, and over a year, it's $480. Now, imagine if you put that $480 into a savings account instead. With compound interest, that money would grow over time, bringing you closer to your long-term financial goals.

Here are a few ways to ensure that your spending decisions support your long-term savings:

- **Track Your Spending:** Keep track of where your money is going each month. You might be surprised by how much you're spending on non-essential items. Once you have a clear picture of your spending habits, you can make adjustments to free up more money for savings.

- **Practice Delayed Gratification:** Instead of buying something immediately, consider whether waiting would allow you to put more money toward your savings. For example, instead of buying a new phone as soon as it's released, wait a few months or until it's on sale. Delaying purchases can help you make smarter financial decisions that benefit your long-term goals.

- **Visualize Your Long-Term Goals:** Keep your long-term savings goals front and center.

Whether it's saving for college, a car, or a trip, having a clear vision of what you're working toward can help you resist unnecessary spending. Every dollar you save brings you one step closer to reaching that goal.

In conclusion, smart spending isn't about depriving yourself—it's about making thoughtful choices that align with your financial goals. By practicing comparison shopping, choosing generic products when possible, avoiding impulse buys, and being mindful of how today's spending impacts tomorrow's savings, you can ensure that you're using your money wisely and building a strong financial future.

CHAPTER 5: BORROWING RESPONSIBLY

What It Means to Borrow Money and Pay It Back with Interest

Borrowing money can be a powerful tool that helps you achieve important life goals, like paying for college, buying a car, or starting a business. However, borrowing comes with the responsibility of paying back what you owe—usually with added interest. Understanding how borrowing works is essential to avoid debt traps and ensure that you're making responsible financial decisions.

When you borrow money from a lender, whether it's a bank, a credit card company, or a family member, you are expected to pay it back. The lender charges interest, which is a fee for allowing you to use their money. **Interest** is usually expressed as a percentage of the loan amount and is paid over time along with the principal (the original amount borrowed). The longer you take to pay back the loan, the more interest you will accumulate.

Here's an example:

- If you borrow $1,000 with an interest rate of 5% per year, you'll owe $50 in interest by the end of the first year. This means your total repayment for that year would be $1,050. If you take longer to repay the loan, the amount of interest you owe continues to grow. It's important to understand this because delaying repayment means paying more money in the long run.

Borrowing responsibly means being aware of how much you're borrowing, what the interest rate is, and how long it will take you to repay the loan. Before taking on any debt, ask yourself: "Do I really need to borrow this money?" and "Can I afford to pay it back on time?"

The Basics of Loans and How They Apply to College, Cars, and Large Purchases

Loans can help you achieve goals that you might not be able to pay for upfront, such as going to college or buying a car. Let's break down the different types of loans you might encounter and how they work:

1. **College Loans**

   College education is one of the most significant investments you can make in your future, but it's also expensive. Many students take out student loans to help cover the cost of tuition, books, and living expenses. These loans usually come with lower interest rates compared to other types of loans, and repayment typically starts after you graduate. However, the longer you take to repay, the more interest you'll accumulate.

   Before taking out a student loan, it's important to research different types of loans—such as federal and private loans. Federal loans often have more flexible repayment options and lower interest rates, making them a better choice for most students. However, even with low interest rates, student loans can add up quickly, so it's crucial to borrow only what you need.

2. **Car Loans**

A car loan allows you to buy a vehicle and pay for it over time. Car loans typically last between 3 to 5 years and come with an interest rate that depends on your credit score (more on that below). When you take out a car loan, the lender expects you to make monthly payments until the loan is paid off. If you miss payments, the lender can repossess your car.

When considering a car loan, think about the total cost of the car, not just the monthly payment. Some dealerships may offer lower monthly payments but extend the loan period, which means you'll pay more in interest over time. It's important to make sure that the car you're buying is within your budget, including insurance, maintenance, and gas.

3. **Loans for Large Purchases**

If you're making a large purchase, like buying a home or starting a business, you may need a personal or business loan. These loans can come with higher interest rates, depending on your credit score and financial history. Before taking out a loan for a large purchase, make sure you fully understand the terms of the loan, including the interest rate, repayment period, and any additional fees.

Borrowing for large purchases can be beneficial, but it also means taking on more debt. The key is to plan ahead, understand how much you can afford to borrow, and ensure that you have a repayment plan in place.

Understanding Credit Scores and How They Affect Your Future Borrowing

Your **credit score** plays a critical role in your ability to borrow money. A credit score is a three-digit number that represents your creditworthiness—essentially, how likely you are to repay a loan on time. Lenders use your credit score to decide whether to lend you money and what interest rate to charge.

Credit scores range from 300 to 850, with higher scores indicating better credit. A higher credit score means you're more likely to get approved for loans and pay lower interest rates. Conversely, a low credit score makes it harder to borrow money, and if you do get approved, you'll likely have to pay a higher interest rate.

Here are some factors that influence your credit score:

- **Payment History:** Making payments on time is the most important factor in determining your credit score. Late payments can significantly lower your score and make borrowing more expensive in the future.

- **Credit Utilization:** This refers to how much of your available credit you're using. If you're maxing out your credit cards or using a large portion of your available credit, it can lower your score.

- **Length of Credit History:** The longer you've been borrowing and successfully repaying debt, the higher your score will be.

- **New Credit Inquiries:** Applying for many new loans or credit cards in a short period can lower your score.

Maintaining a good credit score is essential for borrowing responsibly. The better your credit score, the more options you'll have for borrowing, and the less interest you'll pay over time.

Managing Debt Responsibly and Paying Back on Time

Once you've borrowed money, it's crucial to manage your debt responsibly. This means keeping track of how much you owe, making payments on time, and avoiding taking on more debt than you can handle. Poor debt management can lead to financial stress, lower credit scores, and even legal consequences.

Here are some tips for managing debt responsibly:

1. **Make Payments on Time**

   Always pay at least the minimum amount due by the payment deadline. Missing payments can result in late fees, higher interest rates, and a lower credit score. To stay on top of your payments, set up automatic payments or reminders so you never miss a due date.

2. **Pay More Than the Minimum**

   If you can, try to pay more than the minimum amount required. This helps you pay off your debt faster and reduces the amount of interest you'll pay over the life of the loan. Even paying an extra $20 or $50 a month can make a big difference in reducing your debt.

3. **Create a Debt Repayment Plan**

   If you have multiple debts, create a repayment plan. One popular method is the **debt snowball** approach, where you focus on paying off your smallest debt first while making minimum payments on your larger debts. Once the smallest debt is paid off, you move on to the next smallest, gaining momentum as you go.

Another option is the **debt avalanche** approach, where you prioritize paying off the debt with the highest interest rate first, saving you the most money on interest.

4. **Avoid Taking on New Debt**

   While repaying existing debt, avoid taking on new debt unless absolutely necessary. This will prevent you from falling into a debt cycle where you're borrowing just to keep up with payments. Focus on paying down your current debts before considering new loans or credit.

5. **Seek Help if You're Struggling**

   If you're having trouble managing your debt, don't hesitate to seek help. Many financial advisors, non-profit organizations, and credit counseling services can help you create a debt management plan and negotiate with lenders to reduce interest rates or create more manageable payment schedules.

By borrowing responsibly and managing debt effectively, you can use loans to reach important goals without jeopardizing your financial future. Understanding how loans work, maintaining a good credit score, and paying back on time are essential steps in becoming a financially savvy individual.

CHAPTER 6: PROTECTING YOUR MONEY

Why It's Essential to Safeguard Your Money and Financial Information

You've worked hard to earn your money, and it's important to make sure you keep it safe. In today's world, protecting your money isn't just about locking it in a vault—it also involves safeguarding your financial information. As more transactions happen online and financial data becomes digitized, your personal and financial details can be vulnerable to theft or fraud. Identity theft, scams, and data breaches can lead to significant financial loss and damage to your credit.

Protecting your money and information means taking steps to prevent unauthorized access to your bank accounts, credit cards, and personal data. Whether it's keeping your debit card PIN private or being cautious about where and how you share personal information online, maintaining security is crucial to avoiding financial setbacks.

By adopting smart security practices, you can help prevent fraud, theft, and other financial risks. This chapter will guide you through the best ways to safeguard your money, both online and offline.

Best Practices for Online Safety

In the digital age, protecting your money starts with protecting your online accounts. Every time you log into a bank account, make a purchase online, or share personal information through the internet, you're exposing your financial data to potential risks. By following best practices for online safety, you can significantly reduce the chances of your information falling into the wrong hands.

1. **Create Strong Passwords**

   One of the simplest yet most effective ways to protect your financial accounts is by using strong, unique passwords. Weak passwords, such as "123456" or "password," are easy for hackers to guess. Instead, follow these guidelines for creating strong passwords:

- Use a combination of uppercase and lowercase letters, numbers, and special characters.

- Avoid using easily guessable information like your name, birthdate, or favorite sports team.

- Aim for a password that is at least 12 characters long.

- Use different passwords for each of your accounts. This way, if one password is compromised, your other accounts remain secure.

- Consider using a **password manager** to store and manage your passwords securely. This allows you to create complex passwords without having to remember them all.

2. **Be Cautious of Scams**

Online scams are everywhere, and scammers are always looking for new ways to trick people into giving away their personal or financial information. Here are some tips to help you avoid falling victim to scams:

- **Phishing Scams:** These scams often come in the form of emails or text messages that appear to be from legitimate companies (such as your bank or a well-known retailer). The message might ask you to click on a link and enter your login details, but the link leads to a fake website designed to steal your information. Always verify the sender's identity and never click on suspicious links.

- **Fake Deals and Offers:** Be wary of offers that seem too good to be true, such as emails claiming you've won a prize or can purchase an expensive item at an unbelievably low price. Scammers often use these tactics to get you to share your credit card information.

- **Unsecure Websites:** When shopping or banking online, make sure the website is secure by checking for "https" at the beginning of the web address and a small padlock icon in the address bar. These indicate that the website is using encryption to protect your information.

By following these online safety tips, you can keep your financial information secure and reduce the risk of fraud.

Understanding How Banks Protect Your Money

When you deposit your money in a bank, you can trust that it's being kept safe. Banks are equipped with advanced security measures to protect your funds and ensure that your money is secure, even if something goes wrong. Here's how banks help safeguard your money:

1. **FDIC Insurance**

In many countries, banks are insured by government agencies like the **Federal Deposit Insurance Corporation (FDIC)** in the United States. In Canada, banks are insured by the **Canada Deposit Insurance Corporation (CDIC)**. This means that if your bank were to fail, your deposits would be insured up to a certain amount (typically $250,000 per depositor in the United States and up to $100,000 in Canada as of April 30, 2020). FDIC insurance provides peace of mind, knowing that your money is safe even in the unlikely event of a bank collapse.

2. **Encryption and Security Protocols**

Banks use encryption to protect your information when you access your accounts online or through mobile apps. Encryption scrambles your data, making it unreadable to anyone who tries to intercept it. This ensures that sensitive information like your account numbers, passwords, and transactions are secure.

3. **Two-Factor Authentication (2FA)**

Many banks offer or require **two-factor authentication** (2FA) to add an extra layer of security when you log in. With 2FA, you need to provide two forms of identification: typically your password and a one-time code sent to your phone or email. This makes it much harder for someone to hack into your account, even if they have your password.

4. **Fraud Monitoring and Alerts**

Banks use sophisticated systems to monitor your accounts for suspicious activity. If unusual transactions occur (such as a large purchase in another country), your bank may flag the transaction and send you an alert to confirm whether it was authorized. This helps prevent fraudulent transactions before they happen.

5. **Zero Liability Protection**

Many banks offer **zero liability protection** on debit and credit card transactions, meaning you won't be held responsible for unauthorized charges if your card is lost, stolen, or used fraudulently. However, it's important to report any suspicious activity immediately to ensure you're covered.

These measures allow banks to safeguard your money and ensure that your funds are protected from theft, fraud, and other risks. Understanding how banks protect your money can give you confidence in keeping your savings and earnings in a secure place.

The Importance of Protecting Personal Financial Records

In addition to securing your online accounts, it's equally important to protect your physical financial records. Documents like bank statements, tax returns, and credit card bills contain sensitive information that could be used to steal your identity or access your accounts. Here's how to protect your personal financial records:

1. **Shred Unnecessary Documents**

   Don't just throw away bank statements or documents with personal information—shred them first. This prevents anyone from digging through your trash and finding information that could be used for identity theft. Use a cross-cut shredder for maximum security.

2. Store Important Documents Safely

Keep important financial records, such as tax returns, loan agreements, and insurance policies, in a secure location like a fireproof safe or a locked filing cabinet. This protects them from theft, loss, or damage. If possible, also keep digital copies of these documents as a backup.

3. Be Careful When Sharing Information

Be cautious about sharing your personal or financial information, even with trusted individuals. Only provide information like your Social Security number, bank account details, or credit card numbers when absolutely necessary, and ensure you're sharing it through secure methods.

4. **Monitor Your Credit Report**

   Regularly check your credit report to ensure there's no unauthorized activity, such as accounts opened in your name that you didn't authorize. By keeping an eye on your credit report, you can catch identity theft early and take steps to resolve it quickly.

5. **Safeguard Your Devices**

   Keep your phone, computer, and other devices secure by using passcodes, fingerprint or facial recognition, and antivirus software. If your device is lost or stolen, these security measures can help prevent unauthorized access to your financial accounts.

By taking proactive steps to protect your money, both online and offline, you can reduce the risk of fraud, identity theft, and financial loss. Whether it's creating strong passwords, being cautious of scams, or securing your personal financial records, safeguarding your money is an essential part of managing your finances responsibly.

CHAPTER 7: THE POWER OF GIVING

How Charitable Giving Fits into Your Budget

Giving back is one of the most rewarding ways to use your money, but it's important to plan for it just like any other financial goal. Charitable giving can fit into your budget without jeopardizing your savings or financial responsibilities, and it doesn't have to be a huge amount to make an impact.

The key to incorporating **charitable giving** into your budget is to treat it like any other category of expenses. After covering your needs and setting aside money for savings, you can decide how much you'd like to give. Some people choose to set aside a specific percentage of their income for charitable giving, while others might allocate a fixed dollar amount each month.

For example, you might decide to give 5-10% of your income to a cause you care about. If you earn $100 a week from a part-time job, setting aside $5 to $10 for charitable donations can make a meaningful difference without putting a strain on your finances. If you don't have extra cash to spare, consider other ways to give, such as donating your time or items you no longer need.

By planning for charitable giving in your budget, you can ensure that your generosity aligns with your financial goals and obligations.

The Impact of Giving Back Through Donations, Volunteering, and Community Involvement

Giving back doesn't always mean giving money. There are many ways to make a difference, whether it's through **donations, volunteering, or community involvement**. Each form of giving has its own unique impact and can bring a sense of fulfillment and purpose to your life.

1. **Donations**
   Donating money to a charity or cause you

believe in is a direct way to support organizations that are making a positive impact. Whether it's donating to a local food bank, a medical research foundation, or an environmental organization, your financial contributions help fund important work that can change lives.

In addition to money, you can also donate items such as clothing, books, or electronics. Many organizations accept gently used items and distribute them to those in need. Donating things you no longer use not only helps others but also allows you to declutter and give new life to items that might otherwise go to waste.

2. **Volunteering**

If you don't have the financial resources to give, donating your time is just as valuable. Volunteering allows you to directly contribute to your community while developing new skills and making connections. Whether you're helping at a local shelter, tutoring students, or participating in community clean-up projects, your time and effort can have a lasting impact.

Volunteering also offers a chance to gain new perspectives and experiences that can shape your understanding of the world. It can be a rewarding experience that teaches you about empathy, teamwork, and the importance of giving back.

3. **Community Involvement**

Getting involved in your community can take many forms, from organizing fundraisers to participating in local events that raise awareness for important causes. Community involvement brings people together to work toward a common goal, whether it's improving local schools, supporting small businesses, or advocating for social justice.

By participating in community activities, you contribute to the greater good while also building strong relationships with those around you. The connections you make can lead to future opportunities for collaboration, learning, and personal growth.

Finding Causes You Care About and How Even Small Contributions Make a Difference

Giving back is most meaningful when you support causes that align with your values and passions. Whether you care about the environment, education, healthcare, animal welfare, or social justice, there are countless causes that need support. Finding a cause that resonates with you will make your giving experience more personal and impactful.

To find the right cause, ask yourself:

- What issues am I passionate about?

- What changes do I want to see in the world?

- Which organizations are making a positive impact in my community?

Even small contributions can make a big difference. For example, donating $5 to a hunger relief organization may seem like a small amount, but combined with donations from others, it can help feed multiple families. Similarly, volunteering just a few hours a month can help an organization run more efficiently and expand its services.

No contribution is too small—when many people come together to give, it creates a ripple effect that can lead to real change.

Tithe and Offering: Giving to God

In addition to donating to charitable causes, one of the most important forms of giving for believers is the practice of **tithing** and **offering**—giving a portion of your income back to God through the church. Tithing is rooted in scripture and is considered an act of obedience, faith, and worship. It involves giving 10% of your income to support the work of the church and to honor God for His provision in your life.

The Bible clearly instructs us to tithe:

"Bring the whole tithe into the storehouse, that there may be food in my house. Test me in this," says the Lord Almighty, "and see if I will not throw open the floodgates of heaven and pour out so much blessing that there will not be room enough to store it." (Malachi 3:10, NIV)

This scripture not only calls for us to tithe but also highlights one of the significant benefits of tithing: the promise of God's blessings. By faithfully giving the first 10% of your income to God, you invite His supernatural provision into your life. Tithing teaches us to trust God with our finances, knowing that He is the ultimate provider.

In addition to tithes, **offerings** are another form of giving that goes beyond the tithe. While the tithe is a set amount (10%), offerings are voluntary and given out of a heart of generosity. The Bible encourages believers to give offerings as a way of blessing others and furthering God's kingdom:

"Each of you should give what you have decided in your heart to give, not reluctantly or under compulsion, for God loves a cheerful giver." (2 Corinthians 9:7, NIV)

Offerings can be directed toward church projects, missions, or helping those in need. They are an opportunity to give beyond your tithe as an expression of love, gratitude, and devotion to God.

The Impact and Benefits of Tithes and Offerings

Giving tithes and offerings is not just a financial transaction; it's an act of worship and spiritual discipline that brings both spiritual and practical benefits:

1. **Spiritual Growth and Obedience**

   Tithing is a way of putting God first in your life, including your finances. When you give to God, you acknowledge that everything you have comes from Him. This act of obedience draws you closer to God, deepening your faith and trust in His provision.

2. **God's Blessings and Provision**

   As Malachi 3:10 shows, God promises to bless those who tithe. While these blessings may come in various forms—financial, spiritual, or even relational—faithfully tithing invites God's provision and protection over your finances.

3. **Supporting the Work of the Church**

   Tithes and offerings help fund the work of the church, allowing it to fulfill its mission of spreading the gospel, supporting the community, and helping those in need. The

Bible emphasizes the importance of giving to support God's work:

"Honor the Lord with your wealth, with the firstfruits of all your crops; then your barns will be filled to overflowing, and your vats will brim over with new wine." (Proverbs 3:9-10, NIV)

4. **Cultivating a Generous Heart**

   Giving tithes and offerings fosters a generous spirit within you. It shifts your focus from material things to eternal values and helps you cultivate a heart that cares about God's kingdom and the needs of others.

Tithing and Offering as a Form of Charity

Giving to the church through tithes and offerings can be viewed as a form of **charity giving**, as it supports not only the operational needs of the church but also outreach programs, community aid, and global missions. The church often uses these funds to care for the less fortunate, support missionaries, and provide for various social and spiritual needs within the community.

By contributing to the church, you're not only honoring God but also participating in charitable efforts that make a tangible difference in the lives of others. This aligns with the biblical call to help those in need:

"Whoever is generous to the poor lends to the Lord, and He will repay him for his deed." (Proverbs 19:17, ESV)

Through tithes, offerings, and other forms of charitable giving, you become an active participant in building God's kingdom and making a positive impact on the world around you.

In summary, **tithes and offerings** are a vital part of a believer's financial and spiritual life. They not only honor God but also support the church's mission to serve the community and the world. By giving to God and to others, you cultivate a heart of generosity and experience the blessings of living in alignment with His principles.

Building a Habit of Generosity Early On

Generosity is a habit that can be cultivated from a young age. By incorporating giving into your financial routine early on, you'll develop a lifelong mindset of kindness, empathy, and responsibility toward others. Just as you make it a habit to save and budget, you can also make generosity a regular part of your life.

Here are some ways to build the habit of generosity:

1. **Set Giving Goals**

   Just as you set savings goals, set goals for how much you'd like to give each year. Whether it's a dollar amount, a specific number of volunteer hours, or donating a certain number of items, having clear goals keep you motivated and intentional about your giving.

2. **Give Regularly**

   Instead of waiting for a special occasion to give, consider making it a regular part of your routine. You might set aside a small amount of money each month for donations or commit to volunteering a certain number of hours per year.

Consistent giving not only makes a difference but also keeps you connected to the causes you care about.

3. **Involve Friends and Family**

Giving back can be even more rewarding when shared with others. Encourage your friends and family to join you in supporting a cause, whether it's through a group volunteer project or a charity fundraiser. Not only does this amplify your impact, but it also helps create a culture of generosity within your community.

4. **Reflect on the Impact**

Take time to reflect on how your contributions are making a difference. Whether it's hearing from the organization you support or seeing the positive changes in your community, understanding the impact of your generosity will inspire you to keep giving.

Building a habit of generosity isn't just about making a financial impact—it's about creating a mindset of compassion and service. As you continue to grow and achieve your own financial goals, you'll find that giving back brings a sense of purpose and fulfillment that money alone can't provide.

By including charitable giving in your financial plan, finding causes you care about, and developing a habit of generosity, you can make a positive difference in the world. Giving back not only benefits others but also enriches your own life by connecting you to a greater purpose and community.

WRAP-UP: A ROADMAP TO FINANCIAL SUCCESS

As we come to the end of this guide, let's take a moment to reflect on the essential financial skills you've learned and how they come together to help you achieve lifelong financial success. Mastering these skills will set you on the path to managing your money confidently and making informed decisions that support your goals and dreams.

Recap of the Critical Skills Learned

Throughout this guide, we've explored the seven key areas of financial literacy that form the foundation for managing your money wisely. Let's revisit each one:

1. **Earning**

   The first step to financial independence is

learning how to earn money. Whether through part-time jobs, entrepreneurial ventures, or a future career, earning gives you the resources to achieve your financial goals. By identifying your talents, honing your skills, and seeking opportunities, you can take charge of your income and lay the groundwork for success.

2. **Saving**

Saving is about paying yourself first and setting aside money for future needs. By understanding the difference between short-term, medium-term, and long-term savings goals, you can prioritize your financial objectives and build a cushion for unexpected expenses. You've also learned the power of compound interest and how saving consistently allows your money to grow over time.

3. **Budgeting**

A budget is your financial roadmap. By creating a personalized budget, you can track your income and expenses, differentiate between needs and wants, and ensure you're living within your means. Budgeting allows you to plan for the future, avoid overspending, and set money aside for savings and fun while still covering your essential expenses.

4. **Spending**

   Smart spending means making thoughtful, informed purchasing decisions. By practicing comparison shopping, choosing between brand-name and generic products, and avoiding impulse buys, you ensure that your money is being spent wisely. Your spending habits have a direct impact on your ability to save for long-term goals, so learning to prioritize essential spending is crucial.

5. **Borrowing**

   Borrowing responsibly can help you achieve major goals like going to college or buying a car. However, it's essential to understand how loans work, how interest affects repayment, and the importance of maintaining a good credit score. Managing debt effectively and paying back what you owe on time are key to avoiding financial stress and building a strong credit history.

6. **Protecting**

   Protecting your money and personal information is vital in today's digital world. Whether it's creating strong passwords, avoiding online scams, or safeguarding your financial records, taking steps to secure your assets helps prevent fraud and identity theft. You've also learned how banks work to protect your money through encryption, fraud monitoring, and insurance.

7. **Giving**

   Giving back is an essential part of financial well-being. Whether through donations, volunteering, or community involvement, you can make a meaningful impact on the world around you. By incorporating charitable giving into your budget and building a habit of generosity, you create a positive cycle of helping others while enriching your own life.

These seven skills form a comprehensive approach to financial management that will serve you well throughout your life. They are interconnected and work together to help you achieve financial security and independence.

Encouraging Lifelong Financial Learning and Practice

While this guide provides a strong foundation, financial literacy is a lifelong journey. The world of money is constantly changing, and there's always more to learn. Staying informed about new financial tools, opportunities, and trends will help you continue making smart financial decisions in the future.

Here are some tips for continuing your financial education:

- **Stay Curious:** Seek out books, podcasts, articles, and online courses that can help you deepen your understanding of personal finance. Whether it's learning about investing, retirement planning, or new ways to save, staying curious will help you grow your financial knowledge.

- **Learn from Experience:** As you begin to manage your own money, you'll learn from your successes and mistakes. Take the time to reflect on your experiences and adjust your financial habits as needed. Every financial decision, big or small, is an opportunity to learn and improve.

- **Ask for Help:** Don't hesitate to ask for guidance from financial experts, mentors, or family members. Whether you're looking for advice on budgeting, saving, or investing, seeking help from those with experience can provide valuable insights and help you avoid common mistakes.

By making a commitment to ongoing financial learning, you'll be better prepared to navigate the complexities of managing money in a changing world.

Setting Financial Goals for the Future and Following Through

One of the most important aspects of financial success is setting clear, achievable goals. Whether your goals are short-term (like saving for a concert), medium-term (like buying a laptop), or long-term (like paying for college), having a plan gives you direction and motivation.

Here's how to set financial goals for the future:

1. **Define Your Goals**

   Think about what you want to achieve financially, both in the near future and years down the road. Write down your goals and be specific. For example, instead of just saying "I want to save money," you might set a goal to "save $500 for a summer trip by the end of the year." This clarity helps you stay focused.

2. **Break Goals Into Steps**

   Large financial goals can feel overwhelming, but breaking them down into smaller, manageable steps make them easier to achieve. For example, if you want to save $3,000 for college, calculate how much you need to save each month to reach your goal on time. These smaller milestones will keep you motivated.

3. **Create a Plan**

   Once you've set your goals, create a budget and a savings plan to help you achieve them. Decide how much of your income you can allocate to each goal and track your progress. If necessary, make adjustments along the way to ensure you stay on track.

4. **Stay Committed**

Following through on your financial goals require discipline and persistence. There will be times when it's tempting to spend money on something you don't need or skip a month of saving, but staying committed to your plan will bring long-term rewards. Remember, financial success is a marathon, not a sprint.

5. **Celebrate Your Achievements**

When you reach a financial goal, take time to celebrate your accomplishment. Whether it's reaching a savings target or paying off a loan, recognizing your success will keep you motivated to set and achieve new goals.

By setting and following through on your financial goals, you'll be well on your way to a secure and prosperous future.

Final Thoughts

Financial success doesn't happen overnight—it's the result of consistent learning, practice, and dedication. By mastering the skills of earning, saving, budgeting, spending, borrowing, protecting, and giving, you'll have the tools to manage your money effectively and make informed decisions that align with your goals.

Your financial journey is just beginning. The more you apply what you've learned in this guide, the more confident and empowered you'll become in managing your finances. Remember, every step you take toward financial independence brings you closer to achieving your dreams.

ADDITIONAL RESOURCES

As you continue your journey toward financial success, there are plenty of resources available to help you deepen your understanding and practice your financial skills. From interactive games to expert advice, these tools can make learning about money fun and engaging. Below are some valuable resources that can support your financial education.

Financial Games, Quizzes, and Tools to Practice Financial Skills

Learning about money management doesn't have to be boring! There are several fun and interactive games that allow you to practice the skills you've learned in this guide. These resources will help you test your knowledge while making financial literacy enjoyable.

1. **Financial Football**

Put your financial skills to the test with this NFL-themed game where players answer financial questions to advance down the field and score touchdowns. This fast-paced game covers topics like budgeting, saving, borrowing, and protecting your money. You can play online or with friends and family to see who knows the most about managing money.

Play here: Financial Football

(https://www.financialfootball.com)

2. **Financial Soccer**

Just like Financial Football, this World Cup-themed game challenges your financial knowledge through multiple-choice questions. Learn about smart spending, managing debt, and saving for the future while competing in a virtual soccer match.

Play here: Financial Soccer

(https://financialsoccer.com/en)

3. **Savings Calculator**

Use this simple tool to figure out how your savings can grow over time, especially with the help of compound interest. Whether you're saving for college, a vacation, or a big purchase, this calculator helps you set goals and track your progress.

Try it here: Savings Calculator

(https://www.calculator.net/savings-calculator.html)

4. **Lunch Tracker**

Curious about how much you're spending on lunch each week or month? This tracker helps you calculate your food expenses and identify ways to save. Small changes, like packing your lunch, can add up to big savings over time! Track your spending here: Lunch Tracker

(https://www.practicalmoneyskills.org/en/resources/financial-calculators/family-and-life/lunch-tracker.html)

5. **Budget Builder Tool**

This interactive tool helps you create and manage a personal budget by tracking your income and expenses. Enter your monthly earnings and spending categories and see how small changes can free up more money for savings.

Build your budget here: Budget Builder

(https://itools-ioutils.fcac-acfc.gc.ca/BP-PB/budget-planner)

Useful Links for Students to Learn More About Budgeting, Saving, and Investing

There's always more to learn when it comes to managing money. These websites and resources offer in-depth information on topics like budgeting, saving, and investing, specifically designed for students who want to expand their financial knowledge.

1. **Practical Money Skills**

    This website provides a wealth of information on all things financial, including budgeting, saving, borrowing, and protecting your money. You'll find free educational materials, calculators, and games to help you practice your financial skills.

    Visit here: Practical Money Skills

    (https://www.practicalmoneyskills.com/en)

2. **Khan Academy – Personal Finance**

    Khan Academy offers free, easy-to-follow lessons on personal finance topics such as saving, budgeting, and investing. Their videos and interactive quizzes make it easy to learn at your own pace.

    Visit here: Khan Academy – Personal Finance

    (https://www.khanacademy.org/college-careers-more/personal-finance)

3. **Investopedia**

    Learn the basics of investing, including how the stock market works, the different types of investments, and how to start an investment portfolio. Investopedia provides beginner-friendly guides to help you start building wealth early.

Visit here: Investopedia

(https://www.investopedia.com/)

4. **MyMoney.gov**

This government website offers a comprehensive guide to managing your finances, from saving and investing to understanding credit and loans. It's a great resource for students who want to build a solid financial foundation.

Visit here: MyMoney.gov

(https://www.mymoney.gov/)

5. **NerdWallet**

A trusted source for financial advice, NerdWallet offers tips on saving, budgeting, investing, and even finding the best student credit cards. It's an excellent resource for students who want to make informed financial decisions.

Visit here: NerdWallet

(https://www.nerdwallet.com/)

Advice on Finding Mentors and Financial Literacy Programs

One of the best ways to improve your financial skills is to learn from others who have more experience. Whether it's a parent, teacher, or financial expert, having a mentor can provide you with valuable advice, accountability, and encouragement.

Here's how to find the right mentor or financial literacy program:

1. **Talk to Your Parents or Guardians**

   Your parents or guardians likely have years of experience managing money, and they may be able to offer advice or share personal stories about how they handle their finances. Don't be afraid to ask them for help in setting up a budget, learning about credit, or saving for the future.

2. **Reach Out to Teachers or Counselors**

   Many schools offer financial literacy programs or workshops designed to help students learn about money management. Ask your teachers, school counselors, or career advisors if there are any personal finance classes or events you can attend. These programs can give you the practical skills you need to succeed.

3. **Explore Online Financial Mentorship Programs**

   If you're looking for more in-depth guidance, there are online programs that pair students with financial mentors. Websites like **Junior Achievement** and **Operation HOPE** offer financial literacy programs that include mentoring, workshops, and one-on-one financial coaching.

4. **Join a Financial Club**

   Some schools or community centers offer financial clubs where students can learn about budgeting, investing, and entrepreneurship. These clubs can provide a supportive environment for sharing ideas, asking questions, and learning together.

5. **Follow Financial Experts on Social Media**

   Many financial experts share tips and advice on social media platforms like YouTube, Instagram, and Twitter. Following them can provide you with bite-sized pieces of financial wisdom that you can apply to your everyday life. Some popular financial experts for young adults include Dave Ramsey, Ramit Sethi, and Tiffany Aliche (The Budgetnista).

By finding a mentor or participating in financial literacy programs, you'll gain valuable insights and guidance to help you navigate the world of personal finance with confidence.

Final Note on Resources:

The tools and resources listed above are just the beginning of your financial journey. As you continue to grow and manage your money, you'll discover new opportunities to learn, improve, and make informed financial decisions. Whether through games, online tools, or advice from a mentor, you have everything you need to build a solid foundation for your financial future.

About the Author

Nick Imoru is a dynamic speaker, author, educator, entrepreneur, and consultant based in Canada. He is the President of Achievers Centre, a division of Philips Reliability Consult Inc. Nick's mission is centered on empowering the human spirit through consulting, coaching, connecting and circulating ideas and information. His goal is to inspire, ignite passion, create profit, and make a spiritual impact, ultimately helping individuals bridge the gap between where they are and where they aspire to be.

Nick holds a B.Eng. in Mechanical and Production Engineering and an MSc. in Advanced Technology from the UK. With over 18 years of experience in the Oil and Gas industry, he specializes in Maintenance & Reliability Engineering and is a Certified Maintenance & Reliability Professional (CMRP), reflecting his commitment to excellence in his field.

As the author of over 20 books and numerous articles and research papers, Nick's work spans personal development, spirituality, academia, business, and finance. He is the founder of Achievers Consult, Achievers Centre, and Achievers Publishing, all operating under Philips Reliability Consult Inc.

Nick is happily married to Dr. Margaret and is a proud father of two daughters, Nelly and Myra. His unwavering dedication to personal and professional growth, combined with his entrepreneurial spirit, continues to make a profound impact on individuals and organizations, guiding them towards success and fulfillment.

With a vision to inspire, train, develop, and unlock potential, Nick Imoru is committed to helping individuals and businesses achieve their highest levels of success.

To contact Nick or learn more about Achievers Centre, opportunities, speeches, and seminars, please use the information below:

Email: Nick@achieverscentre.com
Website: www.achieverscentre.com

Books by Same Author

- A Heart for God
- Operating God's Private Lines
- Growing In Life
- Money & Pleasure: Trap of Purpose
- Success Buttons for Life & Academic Excellence
- The Making of Greatness
- Your Best Year Ever
- Nothing Just Happens
- How Did I Become Like This
- Achievers Daily Tonic
- Living in His Fullness: Unveiling the Life, Mission, Death and Triumph of Jesus
- Your Belief System: How Your Thoughts Dictate Your Life
- The Wit & Wisdom of Dr David Oyedepo
- The Tongue: How Your Words Shape Your Destiny

- He Has Said...So We May Boldly Say
- Kings Don't Beg, They Make Decrees
- Character: The Blueprint for a Great Future
- Living in His Light: Understanding Your New Identity in Christ
- Personal & Family Budgeting: Mastering Your Money for Financial Freedom
- Choosing the Right Path: A Career Guide for Teens and Youth
- The 21 Life Rules Every Child Should Live By
- Saving Your Future: A Practical Guide to Financial Literacy
- The Power of Your Environment: How Your Surroundings Shape Your Life
- Think It, Do It: How to Turn Thoughts into Meaningful Action
- Adventures in God's Amazing Storybook, Part 1
- Adventures in God's Amazing Storybook, Part 2

To order any of these books, please visit:

Our online shop @ www.achieverscentre.com

or any of the amazon websites:

www.amazon.ca or www.amazon.com

www.amazon.co.uk, etc